SEA STARS /
ESTRELLAS DE MAR

By Ryan Nagelhout

Traducción al español: Eduardo Alamán

Gareth Stevens
Publishing

ease visit our website, www.garethstevens.com. For a free color catalog of all our
h-quality books, call toll free 1-800-542-2595 or fax 1-877-542-2596.

ary of Congress Cataloging-in-Publication Data

out, Ryan.
rs. English & Spanish]
Estrellas de mar / Ryan Nagelhout.
— (Underwater world = el mundo submarino)
ISBN 978-1-4339-8782-3 (library binding)
1. Starfishes—Juvenile literature. I. Title. II. Title: Estrellas de mar.
QL384.A8N3418 2013
593.9'3—dc23

2012021300

First Edition

Published in 2013 by
Gareth Stevens Publishing
111 East 14th Street, Suite 349
New York, NY 10003

Editor: Ryan Nagelhout
Designer: Katelyn Londino
Spanish Translation: Eduardo Alamán

Photo credits: Cover, p. 1 Nir Darom/Shutterstock.com; pp. 5, 24 (sea) Boris Mrdja/Shutterstock.com;
pp. 7, 9, 24 (fish) vilainecrevette/Shutterstock.com; p. 11 Alex Staroseltsev/Shutterstock.com; p. 13 asharkyu/
Shutterstock.com; p. 15 Darren J. Bradley/Shutterstock.com; p. 17 © iStockphoto.com/Maliketh;
p. 19 totophotos/Shutterstock.com; p. 21 iStockphoto/Thinkstock.com; p. 23 Rodger Jackman/Oxford Scientific/
Getty Images.

Printed in the United States of America

CPSIA compliance information: Batch #CW13GS: For further information contact Gareth Stevens, New York, New York at 1-800-542-2595.

Contents

- -

Contenido

A sea star lives
in the sea.
This is its home.

Las estrellas de mar
viven en el mar.
El mar es su hogar.

It has very strong skin.
This keeps it safe.

Las estrellas de mar
tienen una piel fuerte.
Esto las protege.

7

It often has five arms.
Some have up to 40!

Con frecuencia tienen
5 brazos. ¡Algunas
tienen hasta 40!

9

It can live up to
35 years!

¡Las estrellas de mar
viven hasta 35 años!

It can be many colors.

- -

Pueden tener muchos colores.

There are more than 2,000 kinds. They can live all over the world!

Existen más de 2,000 tipos de estrellas de mar. ¡Pueden vivir en todo el mundo!

15

It doesn't have blood!
It fills with water
to move.

¡Las estrellas de mar
no tienen sangre!
Se llenan de agua
para moverse.

Sea stars are strong!
Its arms can even
grow back!

¡Las estrellas de mar
son muy fuertes!
¡Sus brazos les vuelven
a crecer!

19

It can eat lots of fish
and animals.

Las estrellas de mar
pueden comer muchos
peces y animales.

21

It can push its stomach
out of its mouth.
This is how it eats.

Las estrellas de mar
pueden sacar su
estómago fuera de
la boca. Así comen.

23

Words to Know/
Palabras que debes saber

fish/
(los) peces

sea/
(el) mar

Index / Índice